Teen Voices
Real Teens Discuss Real Problems™

Teens Talk About

Leadership and Activism

Edited by Jennifer Landau

Featuring Q&As with Teen Health & Wellness's Dr. Jan

Rosen
YA
New York

Published in 2018 by The Rosen Publishing Group, Inc.
29 East 21st Street, New York, NY 10010

First Edition

Library of Congress Cataloging-in-Publication Data

Names: Landau, Jennifer, 1961– editor.
Title: Teens talk about leadership and activism / edited by Jennifer Landau.
Description: New York : Rosen Publishing, 2018 | Series: Teen voices: real teens discuss real problems | Audience: Grades 7–12. | Includes bibliographical references and index.
Identifiers: LCCN 2017019528| ISBN 9781508176510 (library bound) | ISBN 9781508176596 (pbk.) | ISBN 9781508176350 (6 pack)
Subjects: LCSH: Leadership. | Leadership in adolescents—Juvenile literature.
Classification: LCC HM1261 .T44 2018 | DDC 303.3/4—dc23
LC record available at https://lccn.loc.gov/2017019528

Manufactured in China

The content in this title has been compiled from The Rosen Publishing Group's Teen Health & Wellness digital platform. Additional original content was provided by Clara MacCarald.

Contents

4 Introduction

8 Chapter 1
**Teens Talk About
Finding Their Mission**

18 Chapter 2
**Teens Talk About
Learning to Lead**

27 Chapter 3
**Teens Talk About
Leading in Their
Community**

34 Chapter 4
**Teens Talk About
Rallying Against
Injustice**

42 Chapter 5
**Teens Talk About
Influential Teachers**

51 **The Teen Health &
Wellness Personal Story
Project**

52 **Glossary**

54 **For More Information**

58 **For Further Reading**

60 **Bibliography**

62 **Index**

Introduction

The bad news: the world can be a difficult place. Poverty keeps people from reaching their full potential. Communities lack necessities like clean water and well-built schools. People treat others badly for who they are or where they come from.

The good news: anyone can make a difference.

Teens don't need money or popularity to help make the world a better place. A willingness to get involved is often enough. But to increase their impact, teens can become leaders. Leaders inspire and motivate other people to do good in the world. Anyone can play that role. There's not one kind of leader, just as there is not one way to lead. Teens can lead by taking a position in an organization or by setting an example through their own behaviors. They may have authority, or they may just have a vision.

What effective leaders do share is a certain set of skills. Communication skills allow teens to spread the word about their cause. Delegating is giving tasks or responsibilities to other people. When teens learn to effectively delegate tasks to people, a group can benefit

When teens take part in volunteer work, they learn new skills and make friends while changing lives for the better.

from the strengths and skills of each member. Leaders take responsibility for fixing problems as they come up. They also take responsibility for helping the members of the group meet their goals.

Businesses need leaders, but so do communities and causes. Volunteering and activism are great ways for teens to take leadership roles in their communities. Volunteering is doing work without pay. The kind of volunteer work teens might do depends on the needs of the community and their own interests. Teens might build houses, clean up streets, or spend time with lonely people.

Teens can work to improve the environment in their communities. They can restore local habitats, plant native species, and beautify their surroundings.

Activism is the act of campaigning for social or political change. There are so many great causes for teens to join. They can fight for justice for a specific group by working for laws that treat everyone equally. They can campaign against climate change by educating people about the environmental impact of their day-to-day choices.

Another way to give back is to teach. A good teacher is also a leader. Perhaps a teacher has overcome great obstacles, which can inspire teens to overcome

Share Your Own Story

The stories you are about to read were submitted by your peers to the Teen Health & Wellness Personal Story Project. Sharing stories is a powerful way to connect with other people. By sharing your story, you can connect with others who are dealing with these challenges. Find more information about how to submit your own story at the end of this resource.

problems in their own lives. Or the way that a teacher acts toward others may present a great example. A supportive teacher can help students become effective leaders themselves.

Leading can change the world, but it also transforms the leader. Helping others is a powerful experience that can fill a teen with pride. Teens get to see the improvements they've made in their community or in someone's life. By dealing with the problems of the world, teens gain a new perspective on themselves.

Chapter 1

Teens Talk About Finding Their Mission

Why are we here? What is the purpose of our lives? Some teens just want to do well in a career and be happy in their personal lives. But others discover a mission. A mission is a calling to go out into the world and work for the greater good.

How do teens find a mission? Often it comes from seeing the world in a new way. Teens can discover their mission through travel, which exposes them to different cultures and environments. But they can also find a sense of purpose in helping others in their own communities.

Missions give teens goals to work toward. One teen's mission could be to protect endangered animals, while another's might be to help a community that lacks adequate housing and schools. Goals can also be as specific as improving the life of a single person in need.

Even though the focus is on something bigger than oneself, having a mission benefits teens, as well. This work can be a source of satisfaction, pride, and happiness. Having a purpose makes life more meaningful.

Many older people enjoy spending time with young people, but teens also benefit from friendships that span generations, as elders have much wisdom to share.

Mark's Story

One summer, a couple of years ago, my youth group and I went on a mission trip to Honduras. We were all very excited because this was the first time for some of us to go overseas. When we got there we were met by two armed Honduran soldiers who protected us for the entire trip. I immediately bonded with one of the soldiers, whose name was Edwin. He was just eighteen, only three years older than I was. As we drove through the city of Tegucigalpa, we saw many homeless people, most of them orphans. We arrived at the college we would be staying at and got to meet the students that went there. The students were training to become missionaries and learning English. That night, and every night thereafter, we would play soccer with them, or should I say watch them play soccer while we ran around trying to keep up.

The next day, we went to work. My group went to build a new house for a homeless woman who had recently lost her husband. This felt nice, but I still didn't feel a huge emotional change because I had not gotten to know the woman very well. Regardless, if I wasn't deeply changed, it still felt good to help someone in great need.

The second day of the trip was the day when I was seriously impacted. Our group went to an orphanage. As soon as we stepped off the bus, a little boy named Eduardo latched on to me, and we never parted ways for the rest of the day. He literally hung on to me the entire day, whether he was standing on my feet when I was walking or riding on my back. He drew me a picture, and I bought a bracelet he had made at the orphanage. I still wear it every day.

When it was time to leave and get on the bus, I had to fight back tears because I had become so attached to this little orphan. Even when I was on the bus, Eduardo kept coming back and putting his hand up to the window for me to grab. He would walk away and then

Doing missionary work at an orphanage is a way to make the residents feel valued and respected. This photo shows Dilma Rousseff, president of Brazil from 2011 to 2016, at an orphanage in the capital city of Brasilia.

come back to do it all again. He never truly left my side until the bus finally pulled out and drove away.

I still carry Eduardo with me every day by wearing the bracelet and carrying his picture in my wallet. My Spanish name in Spanish class is even Eduardo. I will never forget meeting this small child and hope to someday return and see him again.

Joella's Story

I sit here waiting for something to come to me to describe what volunteer work means to me. I check my email and read a letter from my thirteen-year-old cousin. He has just gotten back from a mission trip and vacation. I ask him how it was and he replies, "It was sooo cool. I especially liked doing the volunteer work for all the homeless of New York." He has said it perfectly. While volunteer work often sounds boring and taxing, it never turns out to be so. Helping other people allows someone to see a new perspective and build confidence, and it can even give that person a much-needed boost of hope. And it can do the same to you.

I officially began volunteering at the age of eleven. No, this was not offering to weed the yard or cook dinner for my mother (though I'm sure that would have been appreciated just as much). My first volunteer job was at my old preschool. To give your time or energy or money, you have to be interested in what you are doing. So I began teaching. Ever since I was in second grade I have wanted to be a teacher, though now that I like school less and less, this is changing. Yet, I still love to be with kids. They have a sense of joy that can rarely be found in anyone older. Kids are so innocent to all that surrounds them, and they remind me every day to look at the little things in life. A tunnel in the sand. A piece of folded paper. A Lego castle. They help me see that our lives are beautiful even in the smallest ways.

I just finished my fifth summer at the preschool. It was the third year that I was with the same group of

Teens who enjoy interacting with children can look for opportunities in their community to teach, coach, or mentor younger kids.

kids. It amazes me every time I go to see them just how much they have changed and grown. How quickly life goes by. I feel grateful that I had the opportunity to work with them. The school does not need my help, but it is welcomed. The classes are growing and it never hurts to have someone else around. To me, it does not matter if someone obviously needs help or asks for it. You can always give it. Volunteer work does not have to take place in a different town or country. It can simply be going over to your grandparents and spending time with them. Sometimes I go to visit our next-door neighbor to play harp for her. She sits at home all day, every day, and watches television. I know that just saying hello to her makes her day worthwhile.

I not only notice the benefits of volunteer work for other people, but also for me. This summer, I traveled to our sister city in Mexico with a group of people. I was thrilled to practice my Spanish, meet incredible people, and learn about a new culture. We were there to help at numerous schools and build an even greater connection between our cities. People in the greatest need will open their hearts to you and give you indescribable appreciativeness. I would go back in a second.

Next summer, I plan to go to Latin America for two months to work on a service project. I am sure this experience will be the best yet. I will give my best effort to help as many people in as many ways as I can. Maybe I will teach English, or build something to benefit the town, or take photographs. In doing so, I will learn new skills and encounter new things. Most important, though, I will be making someone's life that much better.

Brian's Story

Every summer I travel to Costa Rica to do community service. We stay on a coastal farm in a small village called Punta Judas, and we sleep in a little hut with no air conditioning and very little running water. The water that is used for cooking, cleaning, and even bathing is collected in a tub on the roof from the rain. If it doesn't rain, we don't get the privilege of taking a shower. The bugs in Costa Rica are relentless, constantly biting any exposed skin; the strongest bug spray I can buy still doesn't keep them off. At night the bugs get even worse. The hut that we stay in has screen doors and windows with holes all over, like Swiss cheese. The holes allow the bugs and other creatures to come and go as they please.

The work we do in Costa Rica includes protecting the endangered sea turtles. At night, we walk up and

Volunteering can provide teens with the chance to visit faraway places and have meaningful experiences, such as helping to protect turtles in Costa Rica.

down the beach looking for turtle tracks in the sand to lead us to the fresh turtle nests. Once a nest is found, the Ping-Pong ball–like eggs are counted and collected. Next the eggs are brought to a hatchery that keeps them safe from poachers and predators. The turtles stay in the hatchery until the entire nest hatches, and once they are born, we carefully transport the baby turtles to the edge of the beach where we guard and guide them during their journey to the ocean.

When we do work for the village school we clean up, paint the walls, and try to fix anything that needs fixing. We also help teach the children English and play games with them in the yard. The homes are constructed out of what looks like sheets of scrap metal, and most of the children's clothes are torn and look like they have never been washed. Yet the children are so happy and always have smiles on their faces.

Experiencing firsthand what it's like to live in a Third World country and observing the conditions the children live in had a tremendous impact on me. Eating rice and beans for every meal, praying for rain to take a shower every day, and getting attacked by bugs every minute really taught me to appreciate the life I have. After living in Costa Rica, the hard parts of life don't seem all that hard. I have learned to value the little things in life a great deal more now, such as having clean clothes and a hot shower. I don't see myself "needing" things as I used to or asking for things that I want. Most kids my age don't understand how nice life really is here in America, and how many other people don't even have half of what they have. Going to Costa Rica made me realize that no matter how much I might think my life is hard, it doesn't compare to the people's lives in Costa Rica.

MYTHS AND FACTS

MYTH Teens are too young to make a difference.

FACT There are so many things teens can do to make the world a better place. They can set an example for their classmates, volunteer, get involved in activism, and much more.

MYTH People are born leaders.

FACT Leadership skills are just that: skills. They can be learned, and they can be improved.

MYTH Activism doesn't do any good.

FACT History provides many examples of activism making a difference, from the struggle for women's right to vote to the fight to end segregation.

Chapter 2

Teens Talk About Learning to Lead

A leader is someone who motivates and inspires others to work toward a goal. Leaders may or may not have a title. The president of the student body is a leader. But so is a teen who inspires her classmates by working hard in school and forming connections with other people.

Want to become a more effective leader? Look for opportunities to practice leadership skills in your school and community. Teens can run for student government. They can join an existing group or start their own. Even if teens can't get a position at the head of the organization, they can volunteer to coordinate an event or run a campaign.

Teens can also work on specific leadership skills. For example, they can look for opportunities to speak in public. There are leadership programs available for more formal training, such as the National Outdoor Leadership School (NOLS). Once you learn how to lead, you'll take your abilities with you anywhere you want to go.

Aaron's Story

They always said the next step was college. After high school, it was a foregone conclusion that there was

Running for student government gives a teen the chance to have a dialogue with fellow students even if he or she isn't elected to office.

only one trajectory for high school graduates to follow. I was not like my typical classmates in this regard, not because I was trying to be some anti-conformist or did not like the prospects of college, but because I plainly was not "mature" enough for my self-imposed expectations at the next level. My ultimate goal would be to attend college, but in order to meet these prospects I needed to figure out how to transform myself from this immature high school graduate into a dynamic, adaptable, and successful college student.

Three qualities, I concluded, obstructed a smooth transition into college: leadership, adaptability, and confidence. Knowing my shortcomings, I sought out a program that would promote these qualities. After some searching, I discovered NOLS, the National Outdoor Leadership School. NOLS, known for taking people of all ages into the most remote places, teaches students to recognize and build on their strengths. Although NOLS had expeditions all over the world, I chose the Australian Outback course. I already felt that the months

Spending time in the wilderness can help teens develop valuable life skills. While backpacking, they can learn how to problem-solve and work together as a team.

of canoeing, backpacking, and learning about aboriginal culture would provide the opportunity to see life from a different perspective—while braving the Outback—and culminate with a more mature adult ready for change.

Once we were flown into the Kimberley region, we spent the next seventy-five days learning how to live in harmony with our environment and survive with only the basic necessities. The Kimberley River, one of the most unpredictable rivers in the world, forced us to work as a team and adapt to any obstacle. By having rotating leaders each day, we had to rise to the occasion and improve the team in our own unique way. Each of us became leaders in order to compose a successful expedition, and by utilizing everyone's strengths we were able to persevere through the Outback and overcome our own personal obstacles. After meeting this challenge, I felt that I could move forward and take on the next step in my life: college.

NOLS allowed me to meet the criteria that I set for myself. I will be attending college for the first time at the age of twenty, determined to succeed at the next level because of my recent accomplishments and even more optimistic of what is to come. Though starting college at that age never seemed plausible before, I'm glad that I took the time off to equip myself with the proper tools for success in and out of the classroom. I look forward to jumping into college life with full vigor and am not only excited about my course decisions, but also thrilled by the extracurricular activities in which I want to be involved. For continued growth and to further hone my skills, involvement will be the key.

James's Story

When I was a child growing up, I always wanted to be big, tough, and strong. I looked up to people who projected this image. So that's the attitude and mentality I took. As the years went on, I became bigger, stronger, and much tougher. I thought I was a total "badass," and with this came confidence. I walked the halls loud and full of confidence, and many teachers called me a

leader, but for the most part it went in one ear and out the other. Fitting the stereotype perfectly, I was a big, strong football player who always found a way to get in trouble and never took school seriously. I carried this mentality through most of my schooling until I hit my sophomore year. One day during sophomore year, after working out with my friend Dylan and his dad Mike, Mr. Mike had a talk with me. He told me I was getting bigger and stronger. He also told me something that would

Trying to act tough or cool doesn't make a teen a good leader. Setting a positive example, and caring about others, are sure signs of leadership.

change my point of view forever. Mr. Mike said, "You know James, it isn't about how strong you are physically and emotionally. It's about how you use your strengths to better yourself and impact others."

I sat awhile and let these words sink in. I even went home and laid in my bed trying to fall asleep and still thought about what he told me. That night I realized something about myself: there was more to me than being a big, tough, strong, macho football player, who was loud and had a lot of friends. Maybe my teachers were right. Maybe I had the potential to do great things and to lead others.

After that night everything changed for me. Returning to school, I started caring about my grades and other people's feelings. I began taking schoolwork more seriously and opened up to people I never thought I would. I could do more with my strengths and natural leadership ability than just be that guy who is good at football and acts up in class.

When I started to show more effort at school, most of my friends did not take me seriously at first. They thought it was a joke and it would not be long before I was back to my old routine. Those who did not know me just didn't believe me when I said I was actually trying to change. As the year went on, more and more people began to accept my goals and support me in my decisions. However, some did think I was only doing this for some sort of notoriety, but they were wrong. I was doing this for self-fulfillment.

I still maintained my tough guy image, but with a nicer and more caring side that most didn't know—or care to know. Now that my years in high school are about to come to a conclusion, I can look back on them and know that a small, simple phrase changed my outlook on life. Those words of guidance given by Mr. Mike helped guide me to reach most, if not all, of my goals, in all aspects of high school and life. I now look back on my four years of high school and know that off and on the field, I put all of my strengths and heart into everything I did and exceeded my own expectations.

Christine's Story

The melodious rising and falling notes of the handbells filled the Shanghai Concert Hall with joy. As the last "ding" echoed through the hall, the bell performers were greeted with long and thunderous applause. Yes, I was one of them, standing on the stage, my heart swollen with pride and my eyes watering with joyous tears. We did it!

The time and effort we had put into practicing, fundraising, and organizing was instantaneously forgotten. Our successful performance made everything seem worthwhile.

Handbell choir has become a pivotal part of my life, and I have grown because of it. In 2011, as one of the youngest members of the Bells of Shaughnessy Hand- bell Choir, it was a brand new activity for me. Actually, playing handbells helped shape me into a person who follows instructions well, excels at being part of a team, and strives to reach her full potential.

Whether participating in a handbell choir or joining a sports team, extracurricular activities provide plenty of opportunities for teens to step up and become leaders.

In 2013, I became vice-captain of the choir. In that role, organizing and preparing for the Chinese concert tour was my foremost duty. Indeed, I enjoyed every moment of it. I was responsible for many of the group's overall activities, including designing the choir's website, communicating with sponsors in China, and organizing the trip schedule. Meanwhile, I needed to practice my solo piece, memorize my emcee script, and rehearse with my peers. From this experience, I learned that being a leader involved more than just knowing how to lead and organize a particular group; rather a leader accepts responsibility, listens to and considers the interests and ideas of others, and deals with situations calmly, thinking critically before reacting.

Reflecting on my handbell career, the Shanghai performance has had a lasting impact on me. Minutes before we went on stage, Fiona, a choir member, began throwing up and almost fainted. Her temperature was forty degrees [104 degrees Fahrenheit] and she was too sick to perform. Handbell performance is most definitely a team event, with each member having an integral part to play. After a short discussion with the conductor, we knew we had to use our substitute for this performance. Acknowledging the fact that we were missing a key member, each chorister put his or her best effort into that performance and staved off a potential disaster. Because of this experience, I realize the importance of teamwork and everyone doing their part. Truly, handbell choir has taught me that crises can be overcome with teamwork.

Teens Talk About Leading in Their Community

A community is a group of people who share a connection. They may live in the same place. A neighborhood is a community, for example. Other communities are made up of people who live apart but share an identity, such as the Muslim or gay community.

Humans are social creatures. We need ties to a larger group. Being part of a community gives teens a sense of belonging and connects them to others who can be supportive. A great way to give back is by becoming a community leader.

Ways to lead in the community are limited only by your time, opportunities, and imagination. Teens can join community groups or volunteer their time. A teen might tutor in academics or coach younger kids in a sport. Other activities could include cleaning up litter, maintaining trails at a nature center, helping at a library, or spending time with pets at an animal shelter. Teens can also raise money to support a cause they believe in.

Some volunteer opportunities teach practical skills, such as how to work on a house. Volunteering improves

Pets need socialization, training, and the chance to play. By volunteering at a shelter, a teen can provide care and companionship to animals in need.

a teen's résumé and may help him or her get a job or enter a specific career. It's also a great way to make new friends. Best of all, taking a leadership role makes your community stronger.

Nathan's Story

I have always wanted to help people in need. So, I decided to shave my head for St. Baldrick's. I learned about St. Baldrick's (an organization that raises money for kids with cancer) from the family company where my mom works. The way St. Baldrick's works is you sign up to get your head shaved and create your own account on their website, and people donate money to you to raise money for kids with cancer. The last time I went to an event for St. Baldrick's, I decided I wanted to take the challenge.

I created my page on their website the day I got braces (the picture was really cheesy). I set a goal to raise 250 dollars. I reached that goal in about a day so I changed it to 500. I didn't reach that goal as fast but in the end I raised about 1,800 dollars. Mainly because I got a 1,000 dollar check from my cousin (he used to be the president of the company).

Before the event I got my picture taken in the paper and got a free hat. After I got my head shaved the hat didn't fit on my head, so I had to adjust it. My head wasn't really smooth—it had tiny little thistles of hair that felt weird. My head felt cold and wet for a few days, too.

After I got my head shaved I wore a button that said, "Ask me why I'm bald." So people would ask me that, even after I told them why. It also felt weird when I had a hat or hood on because of the thistles in my hair. People also kept touching my head.

In conclusion, I shaved my head and raised a lot of money for cancer research for children. If you would like to shave your head for St. Baldrick's, you can go to their website and look for an event in your area. The website is http://www.stbaldricks.org, or you can Google St. Baldrick's Foundation.

St. Baldrick's raises funds for children with cancer by having people offer donations in the name of those willing to shave their heads to support the organization's mission.

Hira's Story

The first time I met him he had facial hair and a huge innocent smile on his face. Max, my art teacher's younger brother, who has special needs, couldn't wait to tell me his name and asked if I would walk him to the school play. When we got to the school theater he sat with his family, and I sat with my friends. While watching the play, he shared all the parts that made him laugh with everyone right way. After that, Max and I saw each other a few times and soon I got to help out with a play that he and other special needs young adults put on twice a year. I spent every Tuesday with him and his friends. In the play, characters showed their feelings right away. I saw a place where joy shined through each person.

"Timea go, I'ma ready!" and other phrases like that soon became a part of my vocabulary. With him things are short, simple, and sweet. Hanging out with Max allows me to see how simple the adult world would be if we could still hang on to some of our "childish" qualities. Max does not spend his time overanalyzing; he goes ahead and does what he wants. Yet he has a powerful understanding of himself. These are all qualities I have learned to strive for in my own life. While swimming this summer with him, we were having a water fight and after a while he was not having fun anymore, so he told me to stop. If I tried to continue he held my hand to make me stop. It is refreshing to meet someone who will totally stop me from hurting him and can stand up for himself on the spot.

Helping those in need offers teens more than the opportunity to give to others. Teens benefit from the relationships they form and can learn a lot about their values and goals in life.

If Max was not a part of my life, I do not think I would be the same person. Now I have no apprehension about fighting against the injustices that I see happening.

The more time I spend with Max, the more I see how perceptive he is. I hope to see some of his qualities in myself as an adult. I want to have eyes full of excitement, a trusting smile, and spontaneous actions.

Ask Dr. Jan

Dear Dr. Jan,
I want to take on a leadership role in one of my school's clubs, but I'm worried about how it might affect my social life and grades. How can I balance extracurriculars, schoolwork, and friendships?
—Eric

Dear Eric,
While parents tend to place a tremendous focus on school and grades, many would argue that one's social life and participation in extracurricular activities are equally important. For children and adolescents, both social competence and participation in extracurricular activities correlate strongly with success in adult life, including academic achievement, reduced substance abuse, and overall emotional well-being. Students who take part in extracurricular activities also develop life interests and leadership skills, which can guide future activism and vocational choices.

The challenge is how to create a balance in your life between school, friends, and extracurricular activities. Here are some suggestions on how to create a full, but manageable schedule.

- School should remain a priority. Calculate how much time you typically need after school for studying and homework.
- Try to get involved in extracurricular activities you are interested in that can also be an opportunity to enrich your social life.
- Create study groups with friends who take the same classes. This gives you a chance to get together with friends, and study groups can be an effective way to prepare for exams and work on projects.
- Leave free time in your schedule so you can relax and decompress.

While balancing priorities can be a challenge, it can also enrich your life and lead to unexpected opportunities now and in the future.

Chapter 4

Teens Talk About Rallying Against Injustice

People need the basics—food, clothing, and shelter, for example—but they also need justice. Injustice is unfair or biased treatment, often based on the identity or origin of the people being discriminated against. Injustice can come out of the way people treat each other. But sometimes a country's laws promote inequality. A government may even support genocide, which is the deliberate destruction of a group of people.

To take a stand against injustice, teens can get involved in activism. They can challenge people's biased behaviors. They can support better laws by lobbying, which is working to influence politicians on a specific issue.

Once you find a cause that's meaningful to you, look for ways to support it. Joining a community of activists can help teens stay engaged and motivated. Keep educating yourself about the issues so that you can educate others. Attend a march or other event. You can post on social media about your cause. Write

The 2016 Toronto Pride Parade, shown here, is one way to celebrate and support the LGBTQ+ community. When teens get involved in causes they believe in, real change can take place.

letters to the newspapers and to your government representatives. Raise your voice so that those who can't speak up can be heard.

Hannah's Story

I recently went to Washington, D.C., for the Rally to Stop the Genocide in Darfur. I have to tell you: It was one of the most exciting and meaningful experiences of my life.

On my last birthday, I committed to help stop the genocide in Darfur as my mitzvah project. I talked to friends and relatives, sold green "Save Darfur" wristbands at my school, and created the artwork that is hanging in the social hall as a way to get people interested in the cause. But the genocide didn't stop and I've been feeling hopeless about Darfur. The rally inspired me and gave me hope. When I was there— surrounded by tens of thousands of people who also want to make a difference and have their voices

A campaign that brings awareness to an important issue may include actions such as rallies and marches. The 2015 Million Women Rise march in London brought attention to male violence against women.

heard—it was so powerful that I really felt like I was saving Darfur.

I heard so many wonderful speakers, including Elie Wiesel and other Holocaust survivors, American Jewish World Service president Ruth Messinger, Olympic gold medalist Joey Cheek, government officials from both parties, religious leaders of different faiths, and Sudanese refugees.

Oh yeah, George Clooney was there, too. When he came onto the stage, I thought my mom was going to faint!

Seriously, all the speakers gave eloquent and moving talks that touched me very deeply and reminded me that, even though I'm still a kid, I have been (and can keep on) making a difference. It was incredible to be with so many others who feel like I do.

The next day, I had an equally great experience. I went with a group from my temple to lobby our senators from Colorado. And I wasn't the only kid. Another glrl, even younger than I am, got to take off from school because this cause is so important to her and her mom. Our first stop was Senator Allard's office, where we met with a staff person who really seemed to hear our message. Then we went to Senator Salazar's office, and as we were talking to his staffer, the senator stopped in. We all got to meet and have our picture taken with him. I believe that our coming all the way from home meant a lot and showed our senators how much we want to save Darfur.

The whole weekend was so powerful it's almost indescribable. I believe the rally pushed the government to take the next step, and I'm glad I was a part of it. I hope that when my kids ask me about Darfur, I can tell them that I helped end a genocide. And I encourage all of you to continue what you are doing or start doing even small things, because in the end, everything will make a difference. I am saving Darfur, and you can, too!

Jacob's Story

We are the shoes. We are the last witnesses.

We are the shoes from grandchildren and grandfathers, from Prague, Paris, and Amsterdam, and because we are only made of fabric and leather, not blood and flesh, each one of us avoided the hellfire.

I had heard stories, seen pictures, and even heard survivors' testimonies, yet nothing prepared me for a room full of real, genuine shoes, worn by those people whom we had all heard about. Sure, hearing about millions of shoes piled up is shocking. However, actually walking between the black piles, smelling the damp leather, and imagining the people who wore them was truly a knockout moment.

From March 18 to 21, I went on a Holocaust Awareness and Anti-bigotry Mission to Washington, DC. The trip itself was incredible, but going to the National Holocaust Memorial Museum was clearly the high point. Imagine all the stories you hear and pictures you see about the Holocaust, except everything is real. Genuine artifacts from the camps and the ghettos were just some of the objects that shook me to the core.

One artifact brought me to tears. I've always imagined what it would be like being caged in a cattle

This photo shows the Portrait Gallery of the Holocaust Museum in Washington, DC. Activism doesn't just have to be about current events. Teens can spread the word about past injustices, too.

car on the way to the camps, but the minute I stepped into that rusty red car of death, everything hit me. It took a second to sink in, but when I took a breath and looked around, I literally felt like I had just been hit by a train. All I can say is I knew I was standing on hundreds of lives that had once been in anguish. I can't describe the smell. I felt like I was suffocating, but I needed to stay in that car and take it all in. For many minutes I stood looking over every inch of that tiny cattle car. I saw the barbed wire-covered windows, the dirty wood floor that once held corpses and living bodies alike, and I also saw images. Images of the people crying out in desperation, trapped in the exact spot I was standing. I said a quick Kaddish, the Hebrew prayer of mourning, and I walked out. My eyes were watery as I left to go look at the Zyklon B canister hanging on the wall of the next room.

As I write this, it is the holiday of Pesach, known as Passover. Passover is cause for celebration for us Jews. However, when I think of the holiday when we celebrate our freedom from intense oppression, I now think of the millions of Jews in the camps during the Holocaust. In my mind, I would not have been happy to celebrate freedom when I had none. So I do celebrate Pesach with much happiness, and I'm grateful for the freedom I have, however as I'm celebrating, I think of my ancestors, trapped in the death camps. They had no freedom while others were celebrating. Now I always will remember those who were—and are—not as privileged as I am.

Freedom comes with a price. This price is not measured in funds, but rather in lives and stories. Still today, some people have no freedom, and no reason to celebrate. So on Pesach, I ask you: Have fun and

WHOM TO CALL

The following organizations can help teens find a volunteer position that matches their skills and interests:

Idealist
https://www.idealist.org
Twenty-four hours a day, seven days a week

Volunteer Match
http://www.volunteermatch.org.
Twenty-four hours a day, seven days a week

Points of Light
(800) Volunteer
http://www.pointsoflight.org
Monday through Friday, 9 a.m. to 5 p.m., EST

Volunteen Nation
http://www.volunteennation.org.
Twenty-four hours a day, seven days a week.

be thankful we're free, but also keep in mind that some people do not know true freedom. Remember your ancestors who were trapped in the tentacles of hatred and oppression, and remember that freedom is a right that comes with responsibility. We need to pay the price and make a small sacrifice. In the same way we dip our fingers in our wineglasses at each seder, and take a little out at the mention of each plague, take a little of your own celebratory pleasure away, and dip your finger in the metaphorical wineglass of your life. Take a little out, so the ones who never had freedom at least are remembered, and live on in our words and our deeds.

Shabbat shalom.

Chapter 5

Teens Talk About Influential Teachers

Teachers do more than help kids learn their ABCs. A teacher can change the course of a student's life. A great teacher can act as a friend, a cheerleader, or a role model.

Not only can a great teacher inspire teens to do their best, she can help teens reach their full potential. All teens need someone to believe in them. A teacher's excitement for his subject matter is infectious and can make even a dry topic come alive. Teachers can teach life skills, including leadership skills. They can model being responsible and having a strong work ethic.

Teachers can help students become leaders. A teacher might recommend organizations for teens to join, like a social club, a sports team, or a leadership program. She can be a resource for teens as they grow into leadership roles.

Teens who want to be teachers themselves don't have to wait until after college. Schools and communities provide many opportunities, from tutoring

An effective teacher takes the time to listen to his or her students and focus on their interests and personal goals, as well as their educational needs.

43

classmates to helping with a class of younger kids. Local community centers may have summer positions. The greatest compliment you can give a teacher who has influenced you in a positive way is to influence the lives of your own students.

Sophia's Story

"You don't plan to eat that doughnut, do you?"

Mrs. Brown turns in disgust as I cross the threshold of City Ballet early one Saturday morning.

I scamper to dispose of the evidence and begin the regimen of wrapping my feet by pulling out my tool kit: paper towels, check; tape, check; lamb's wool, check.

Her voice plays in my head, "You must feel the box to know how to manipulate it. No toe gel pads for the girls in this company." I hope I don't lose the toenail I am nursing. The ballet studio is a familiar place filled with ease and complication. A gust of hot air covers me, with the lingering smell of sweat. The dance studio is my home. I take my position at the bar and await my daily dose of discipline.

Mrs. Brown commands my full attention and demands my very best. I imagine what she must have looked like at my age. How did she move? I would give anything to have seen her dance. Now she is frail, weakened and crippled from an unrelenting Parkinson's disease. The volume of her voice is strained, but it is packed with authority and I listen carefully to her instruction. I want to please her, make her proud, and perform to my full potential. She means business, and dance is her business. For her, it means more than moving. It is a way of life, her salvation, her entire world.

Mrs. Brown is from a cultured home filled with music, singing, and abundant love. At nine, she took her first dance class and this experience opened a dream beyond her wildest imagination. Her life changed dramatically at age sixteen when her father was ripped from her life by the Nazis. She retaliated by enlisting in the French Resistance. The next fifty-five years would be filled with lies and betrayal to everyone—even herself and her husband.

She promised him she would keep her Judaism a secret and left every aspect of her life behind—except dance. Dance became her solace, her world, and her only escape. She began teaching young American girls in her bedroom, moving the mattress out by day to create a studio. Her reputation grew and grew; City Ballet was born. Mrs. Brown created a world where girls were able to express themselves through dance. For decades she has provided young girls like me with a safe place to explore self-expression and grow in self-confidence.

Growing up in City Ballet has meant more than maturing year after year; it has been a place of self-discovery. Unlike Mrs. Brown, my family didn't keep my struggles a secret. Fortunately, my learning needs were discovered at an early age and remediation was embraced. Dance became part of the prescription for my ailment. Through movement I learned the discipline of sequencing, repetition, and taking correction. In time, dance became part of my therapy. The cadence of class

Influential teachers can be found both in and out of the classroom. An instructor who guides a student as he or she pursues a passion offers lessons that can last a lifetime.

was predictable and comforting. Mrs. Brown became my compass.

I sat in the sanctuary awaiting Mrs. Brown's most honorable performance. After fifty-five years of secrecy she bravely climbed the stairs of the bima to present her granddaughter with her father's tallit (prayer shawl), her first public expression of her faith. She softly trembled as she spoke, "I'm wrapping you in my father's tallit. His life ended in Auschwitz in early 1942. I thank you for making it part of the future; I love you. Mazel Tov." What courage it took for her to stand before the world. I learned that day that Mrs. Brown was human and flawed. She was finally free and we had one more thing in common: our faith.

Purposefully, I take my place in front of her director's chair, knowing I get more correction there. When I enrolled at age three there was no way I could've imagined all the life lessons that I would learn from Mrs. Brown. All the bleeding toes, blisters, sore muscles, and at times a bruised ego, empowered me to grow in dance and deal with my learning issues. Mrs. Brown never allowed me to compromise. Instead, she drove me to succeed.

The lessons I have learned through struggle, sacrifice, dedication, and perseverance prepare me for the next act: my entrance into college. Mrs. Brown taught me to touch heaven with every movement and to love the person I have become. Although I won't be standing at the bar in front of her chair, she is with me.

Trevor's Story

One person who has strongly impacted my life was my junior English teacher, Mrs. Rivers. She was an amazing, hard-working teacher who taught me to see the brighter side of things. She also did her job exceptionally well, and because of her, my ACT English scores increased dramatically. I would never have come close to getting the score that I did without her. Another thing she did amazingly well was lead by example. Her hard work was like something I had never seen. She was determined to do her work and to do it well. Mrs. Rivers was a hard teacher, but her class never felt harsh; her humor kept the class bright.

Mrs. Rivers's view on life was simply great and contagious in a way. Before I had her, I would always act "oh, woe is me" and never laugh about the bad things that happened in the past. However, one thing she said many times when telling a story was, "Better to laugh about it than cry about it." I learned that little lesson from her, and because of that one saying, I am happier about things that happened in the past. Now I can laugh about almost anything that happened to me. She was a very challenging teacher. She would push us and she would try to get us to better ourselves, and I believe she did a wonderful job.

Mrs. Rivers's teaching was great. She worked extremely hard and always kept us busy in class, yet relaxed outside of class. She would push me further in the classroom, and that greatly improved my English skills. I had never had a teacher push me as hard as she did. I always thought that I was overworked, or had too much work to do in English class. However, the truth was, I never had a teacher push me very much, or give work that was a challenge. But Mrs. Rivers did. She pushed me in that class, she showed me my true potential, and she always led by example with her work ethic. She would get things done, and she would make time to do it. It reminds me of something my dad said to me, "You don't find time, you make time." Even though I never heard Mrs. Rivers say that, I'm sure she would agree with my dad.

A teacher's greatest reward is a student who goes on to succeed on exams, in the workforce, and in his or her personal relationships.

Mrs. Rivers was unquestionably the greatest teacher I have ever had. I hope to one day have another teacher who will push me as hard as she did, one who will not only push me to better myself, but also lead by example. I hope to have a teacher who will do everything that he or she can to make sure everyone understands the material. Mrs. Rivers is quite possibly the best teacher out there, and she is the person I have to thank for my English ACT scores. If only every teacher could be like her.

10 Great Questions
to Ask a Leader You Admire

1. How did you discover what issues you are passionate about?

2. What made you want to take on a leadership role?

3. What qualities make an effective leader?

4. How did you develop your leadership skills?

5. What is the most rewarding part of being a leader?

6. What is the hardest part of being in charge?

7. Who are some leaders you admire?

8. How can I figure out if I'd make a strong leader?

9. If I want to get involved in a cause, where do I start?

10. Are there certain subjects I should take in school to help me become an effective leader?

The Teen Health & Wellness Personal Story Project

Be part of the Teen Health & Wellness Personal Story Project and share your story about successfully dealing with or overcoming a challenge. If your story is accepted for online publication, it will be posted on the Teen Health & Wellness site and featured on its homepage. You will also receive a certificate of achievement from Rosen Publishing and a $25 gift certificate to Barnes & Noble or Chapters.

Sharing stories is a powerful way to connect with other people. By sharing your story, you can connect with others who are dealing with these challenges. Visit teenhealthandwellness.com/static/personalstoryproject to read other teens' stories and to submit your own.

Scan this QR code to go to the Personal Story Project homepage.

Glossary

aboriginal Related to the native people of a place.

activism The act of campaigning for social or political change.

bima The platform from which scripture is read in a Jewish house of worship.

Darfur A province in Sudan that has suffered from war and genocide.

delegating Giving certain tasks or responsibilities to other people.

expedition A journey taken with a certain purpose in mind, such as collecting scientific information or fighting a war.

genocide The deliberate destruction of a group of people, often because of their race or ethnicity.

Hebrew The language of the ancient Jewish tribes.

Holocaust The Nazis' mass killing of millions of Jews and others during World War II.

injustice Unfair or biased treatment of people.

kaddish A Jewish prayer for the dead.

lobbying Working to influence government officals on a specific issue.

mazel tov A Jewish expression meaning congratulations or good luck.

mitzvah A good deed in the Jewish faith.

Parkinson's disease A progressive disease of the nervous system that affects the way people's bodies move.

Pesach A Jewish holiday lasting seven or eight days that celebrates the escape of the Jews from slavery in Egypt; also known as Passover.

predators Animals that hunt other animals in order to eat their flesh.

seder A ceremonial dinner at the beginning of Passover.

Shabbat Shalom A Hebrew wish for someone to enjoy peace on the Sabbath, a day of religious observance for Jews.

sponsors People who give money or support to a particular project.

tallit A Jewish prayer shawl with fringes on each corner.

Zyklon B A poison used by the Nazis to kill people during the Holocaust.

For More Information

AmeriCorps
250 East Street SW
Washington, DC 20525
(800) 942-2677
Website: https://www.nationalservice.gov/programs
    /americorps
Facebook: @americorps
Twitter: @AmeriCorps
Instagram: @americorps
AmeriCorps is a government program that connects
    Americans aged seventeen and up with service
    positions helping communities, people, and the
    environment.

Canadian Student Leadership Association
2460 Tanner Road
Victoria, BC V8Z 5R1
Canada
(902) 880-3121
Website: https://studentleadership.ca
Facebook: @CanadianStudentLeadershipAssociation
Twitter: @CSLA_Leaders
The Canadian Student Leadership Association is a
    charity that promotes leadership development in
    secondary schools across Canada.

Habitat for Humanity International
270 Peachtree Street NW, Suite 1300

Atlanta, GA 30303
(800) 422-4828
Website: http://www.habitat.org
Facebook: @habitat
Twitter: @Habitat_org
Instagram: @habitatforhumanity
Habitat for Humanity helps people build or improve their
    own home with help from volunteers and affordable
    payment plans.

National 4-H Council
7100 Connecticut Avenue
Chevy Chase, MD 20815
(301) 961-2800
Website: http://4-h.org
Facebook: @4-h
Twitter: @4H
Instagram: @national4h
With organizations throughout the United States, 4-H
    builds leadership skills in youth by providing
    opportunities and experiences in different fields.

NOLS
284 Lincoln Street
Lander, WY 82520
(800) 710-6657
Website: https://www.nols.edu/en
Facebook: @NOLS
Twitter: @NOLSedu
Instagram: @nolsedu
NOLS, which began as National Outdoor Leadership

School, is a nonprofit wilderness school that teaches outdoor skills and leadership.

Teen Health and Wellness
29 East 21st Street
New York, NY 10010
(877) 381-6649
Website: http://www.teenhealthandwellness.com
App: Teen Hotlines
Teen Health & Wellness provides nonjudgmental, straightforward, curricular and self-help support on topics such as diseases, drugs and alcohol, nutrition, mental health, suicide and bullying, green living, and LGBTQ issues. Its free Teen Hotlines app provides a concise list of hotlines, help lines, and information lines on the subjects that affect teens most.

Volunteer Canada
275 Bank Street, Suite 400
Ottawa, ON K2P 2L6
Canada
(800) 670-0401
Website: https://volunteer.ca
Facebook: @VolunteerCanada
Twitter: @VolunteerCanada
Volunteer Canada works to increase and support volunteerism and civic participation in Canada

Youth Volunteer Corps (YVC)
1025 Jefferson Street
Kansas City, MO 64105

(816) 472-9822
Website: https://www.yvc.org
Facebook: @youthvolunteers
Twitter: @YVolunteerCorps
YVC is a network of organizations that aims to get youth
    between the ages of eleven and eighteen involved in
    volunteer service.

Websites

Because of the changing nature of internet links, Rosen
Publishing has developed an online list of websites
related to the subject of this book. This site is updated
regularly. Please use this link to access this list:

http://www.rosenlinks.com/TNV/Lead

For Further Reading

Byers, Ann. *Internship and Volunteer Opportunities for People Who Love Animals* (A Foot in the Door). New York, NY: Rosen Publishing, 2013.

Covey, Sean. *The 7 Habits of Highly Effective Teens*. New York, NY: Touchstone, 2014.

Furstinger, Nancy. *Women and Leadership* (A Young Women's Guide to Contemporary Issues). New York, NY: Rosen Publishing, 2013.

Harmon, Daniel. *Internship and Volunteer Opportunities for Science and Math Wizards.* (A Foot in the Door). New York, NY: Rosen Publishing, 2013.

La Bella, Laura. *Internship and Volunteer Opportunities for People Who Love to Build Things* (A Foot in the Door). New York, NY: Rosen Publishing, 2013.

Lowery, Zoe. *The Darfur Genocide* (Bearing Witness: Genocide and Ethnic Cleansing in the Modern World). New York, NY: Rosen Publishing, 2013.

Lowery, Zoe. *The Nazi Regime and the Holocaust* (Bearing Witness: Genocide and Ethnic Cleansing in the Modern World). New York, NY: Rosen Publishing, 2013.

Roza, Greg. *Internship and Volunteer Opportunities for People Who Love Nature* (A Foot in the Door). New York, NY: Rosen Publishing, 2013.

Skeen, Michelle, Matthew McKay, Patrick Fanning, and Kelly Skeen. *Communication Skills for Teens: How to Listen, Express, and Connect for Success* (The Instant Help Solutions). Harbringer, CA: Instant Help, 2016.

Stone, Tanya Lee. *Girl Rising: Changing the World One Girl at a Time*. New York, NY: Wendy Lamb Books, 2017.

Sunseri, Sophia. *Working as a Teacher in Your Community* (Careers in Your Community). New York, NY: Rosen Publishing, 2013.

Thompson, Laurie Ann. *Be a Changemaker: How to Start Something That Matters*. Hillsboro, OR: Simon Pulse/ Beyond Words, 2014.

Whitman, Sylvia. *The Milk of Birds*. New York, NY: Atheneum Books for Young Readers, 2014.

Bibliography

"Aaron's Story." Teen Health and Wellness, October 2016. http://www.teenhealthandwellness.com /article/203/10/aarons-story.

"Brian's Story." Teen Health and Wellness, January 2017. http://www.teenhealthandwellness.com /article/347/11/brians-story.

"Christine's Story." Teen Health and Wellness, October 2016. http://www.teenhealthandwellness.com /article/203/15/christines-story.

Cook-Deegan, Patrick. "How to Help Teens Find Purpose." Greater Good: The Science of a Meaningful Life, April 16, 2015. http://greatergood .berkeley.edu/article/item /how_to_help_teens_find_purpose.

Habitat for Humanity. "Benefits of Volunteering." 2017. http://www.habitat.org/stories /benefits-of-volunteering.

Hannah's Story." Teen Health and Wellness, October 2016. http://www.teenhealthandwellness.com /article/203/9/hannahs-story.

"Hira's Story." Teen Health and Wellness, January 2017. http://www.teenhealthandwellness.com /article/347/12/hiras-story.

"Jacob's Story." Teen Health and Wellness, June 2015. http://www.teenhealthandwellness.com/article/281/9 /jacobs-story.

"James's Story." Teen Health and Wellness, October 2016. http://www.teenhealthandwellness.com

/article/203/11/jamess-story.

"Joella's Story." Teen Health and Wellness, January 2017. http://www.teenhealthandwellness.com /article/347/10/joellas-story.

"Mark's Story." Teen Health and Wellness, January 2017. http://www.teenhealthandwellness.com/article/347/9 /marks-story.

"Nathan's Story." Teen Health and Wellness, January 2017. http://www.teenhealthandwellness.com /article/347/8/nathans-story.

School-Based Health Alliance. "Developing Youth Leadership Skills." Retrieved March 17, 2017. http:// www.sbh4all.org/training/youth-development/youth -engagement-toolkit /developing-youth-leadership-skills.

"Sophia's Story." Teen Health and Wellness, October 2016. http://www.teenhealthandwellness.com /article/292/13/sophias-story.

"Trevor's Story." Teen Health and Wellness, October 2016. http://www.teenhealthandwellness.com /article/203/12/trevors-story.

Index

A

aboriginal culture, 21
activism, 5–6

B

Bells of Shaughnessy hand-bell choir, 24–26
building a home, 10

C

children with cancer, fundraising for, 28–30
college, preparing for, 18–21, 47–49
communication skills, 4
communities
 fundraising for children with cancer, 28–30
 needs of, 5
 volunteering with preschool, 12–13
Costa Rica, and helping sea turtles, 14–16

D

dance, and learning discipline, 44–47
Darfur, rally against genocide in, 35–38
delegating, defined, 4–5

E

environment, helping the, 15–16

F

friendship and "cool" image, 22–24
fundraising, 24, 27, 28–30

G

genocide, 35–38
goals, 4

H

Holocaust
 National Holocaust Museum, 38–41
 survivors, 37, 45–47
Holocaust Awareness and Anti-bigotry Mission, 38
Honduras, and mission to build a house, 9–11

I

image and attitude, 22–24
injustice
 activism against, 34–41
 advocating for equality, 6
 against people with special needs, 32

L

leadership
  described, 4–5, 18
  by example, 49
  skills, developing, 20–21
  stories about, 18–26
lobbying to end injustice,
  34, 37

N

National Holocaust
  Museum, 38
National Outdoor
  Leadership School
  (NOLS), 18, 20

O

orphanage in Honduras,
  10–11
Outback, the, 20–21

P

Parkinson's disease, 44
Pesach (Passover), 40–41
Punta Judas, Costa Rica, 14
purpose, having a sense of,
  8–9

R

Rally to Stop the Genocide
  in Darfur, 35–38

S

St. Baldrick's fundraiser,
  28–30
sea turtles, protecting,
  15–16
special needs students,
  31–32
student government, 18

T

teachers
  of ballet, 44–47
  of English, 47–49
  as influential leaders, 6–7,
    42–49
  tutoring and other opportu-
    nities, 42–44
  volunteering at preschool,
    12–13
teamwork, 26
Teen Health & Wellness
  Personal Story Project,
  7, 51
Tegucigalpa, Honduras, 10

V

visiting neighbors, 14
volunteering
  and activism, 5
  benefits of, 14

About the Editor

Jennifer Landau is an author and editor who has written about psychological bullying, cybercitizenship, and drug and alcohol abuse, among other topics. She has an MA in English from New York University and an MST in general and special education from Fordham University. Landau has taught writing to young children, teens, and seniors.

About Dr. Jan

Dr. Jan Hittelman, a licensed psychologist with over thirty years of experience working with children and families, has authored monthly columns for the *Daily Camera*, Boulder Valley School District, and online for the Rosen Publishing Group. He is the founder of the Boulder Counseling Cooperative and the director of Boulder Psychological Services.

Photo Credits

Cover Diego G Diaz/Shutterstock.com; p. 5 Kathy Hutchins /Shutterstock.com; p. 6 Hero Images/Getty Images; p. 9 sjgh /Shutterstock.com; p. 11 Evaristo Sa/AFP/Getty Images; p. 13 Robert Kneschke/Shutterstock.com; p. 15 Michal Sarauer/Shutterstock.com; p. 19 Chris Clinton/Taxi/Getty Images; p. 20 Joel Rogers/Corbis Historical/Getty Images; p. 22 Thomas Barwick/Taxi/Getty Images; p. 25 © iStockphoto.com/justosolove; p. 28 Denise Truscello/ WireImage/Getty Images; p. 30 Mindy Small/FilmMagic/Getty Images; p. 32 FatCamera/E+/Getty Images; p. 35 Shawn Goldberg /Shutterstock.com; p. 36 Mike Kemp/Corbis News/Getty Images; p. 39 Elan Fleisher/LOOK-foto/LOOK/Getty Images; p. 43 Purestock /Getty Images; p. 46 Thomas Barwick/Stone/Getty Images; p. 49 asiseeit/E+/Getty Images; interior pages graphic elements natt/ Shutterstock.com.

Design and Layout: Nicole Russo-Duca; Photo Research: Ellina Litmanovich